Emergency And Disaster Plan Template

Emergency And Disaster Plan

Mary Oquendo And Kate Klasen

9 780982 883181

This manual provides guidance for a general all-hazards management, using emergency and emergency related agencies, to help pet businesses meet it's responsibilities before, during, and after an event. This manual does not guarantee business, person, or pet's safety.982

ISBN: 978-0-98298831-8-1

TABLE OF CONTENTS

BUSINESS INFORMATION

BUSINESS: _____

WEBSITE: _____

EMAIL: _____

PHONE: _____

ADDRESS: _____

STATE/ZIP CODE _____

OWNER _____

EMAIL: _____

PHONE: _____

ADDRESS: _____

TEAM MEMBER _____

EMAIL: _____

PHONE: _____

ADDRESS: _____

TEAM MEMBER _____

EMAIL: _____

PHONE: _____

ADDRESS: _____

TEAM RESONSIBILITIES

NAME
_____

PHONE TREE
_____

SCHEDULING TRAINING
_____

ROTATING SUPPLIES
_____

DAILY PROCEDURES
_____

CODE RED SIGN UP ALERTS
_____

TRAINING
_____

NAME
_____

PHONE TREE
_____

SCHEDULING TRAINING
_____

ROTATING SUPPLIES
_____

DAILY PROCEDURES
_____

CODE RED SIGN UP ALERTS
_____

TRAINING
_____

NAME
_____

PHONE TREE
_____

SCHEDULING TRAINING
_____

ROTATING SUPPLIES
_____

DAILY PROCEDURES
_____

CODE RED SIGN UP ALERTS
_____

TRAINING
_____

LOCATION OF CRITICAL ITEMS

CASH

COMPUTER BACK-UPS

ELECTRIC SHUTOFF

EMERGENCY SUPPLIES

EVACUATION SUPPLES

FINANCIAL INFORMATION

FIRE EXTINGUISHERS

FIRST AID KITS

GAS SHUT OFFS

GENERATOR/GAS CAN

INSURANCE POLICIES

KEYS

LOCKBOXES

PHOTOS

SAFE HIDING PLACES

SECURITY CAMERAS

SIGNAGE

WATER SHUTOFFS

LOCATION OF
HAZARDOUS MATERIALS

AEROSOL CANS

ALCOHOL

BLEACH

BATTERIES

CHARGERS

CLEANERS

DISINFECTANTS

ELECTRONICS

FERTILIZERS

FLEA AND TICK

FIRE EXTINGUISHER

FRAGRANCES

GAS FOR GENERATOR

GLUE

NAIL POLSH

PAINT

PESTICIDES

PLASTICS

TOILET/MILDEW CLEANERS

TONER

EMERGENCY CONTACTS

NAME : _____

EMAIL : _____

ADDRESS : _____

PHONE : _____

NAME : _____

EMAIL : _____

ADDRESS : _____

PHONE : _____

NAME : _____

EMAIL : _____

ADDRESS : _____

PHONE : _____

NAME : _____

EMAIL : _____

ADDRESS : _____

PHONE : _____

EMERGENCY CONTACTS

NAME : _____

EMAIL : _____

ADDRESS : _____

PHONE : _____

NAME : _____

EMAIL : _____

ADDRESS : _____

PHONE : _____

NAME : _____

EMAIL : _____

ADDRESS : _____

PHONE : _____

NAME : _____

EMAIL : _____

ADDRESS : _____

PHONE : _____

EMERGENCY CONTACTS

NAME :

EMAIL :

ADDRESS :

PHONE :

NAME :

EMAIL :

ADDRESS :

PHONE :

NAME :

EMAIL :

ADDRESS :

PHONE :

NAME :

EMAIL :

ADDRESS :

PHONE :

MUTUAL AID AGREEMENTS

NAME : _____

EMAIL : _____

ADDRESS : _____

PHONE : _____

NAME : _____

EMAIL : _____

ADDRESS : _____

PHONE : _____

NAME : _____

EMAIL : _____

ADDRESS : _____

PHONE : _____

NAME : _____

EMAIL : _____

ADDRESS : _____

PHONE : _____

Open for Business Worksheet
Insurance Coverage Discussion Form

Use this form to discuss your insurance coverage with your agent. Having adequate coverage now will help you recover more rapidly from a catastrophe.

Insurance Agent: _____

Address: _____

Phone: _____ Fax: _____ Email: _____

INSURANCE POLICY INFORMATION

Type of Insurance	Policy No.	Deductibles	Policy Limits	Coverage (General Description)

Do you need Flood Insurance?	Yes __	No __
Do you need Earthquake Insurance?	Yes __	No __
Do you need Business Income and Extra Expense Insurance?	Yes __	No __

Other disaster-related insurance questions:

_____

_____

_____

Passwords

Website	Login	Password

Sensitive Passwords

Website	Login	Password

EMPLOYEE NEEDS

NAME OF EMPLOYEE
_____

EMERGENCY CONTACT
_____

EMAIL:
_____

PHONE:
_____

ADDRESS:
_____

TRAINING

NEED
_____

NAME OF EMPLOYEE
_____

EMERGENCY CONTACT
_____

EMAIL:
_____

PHONE:
_____

ADDRESS:
_____

TRAINING

NEED
_____

NAME OF EMPLOYEE
_____

EMERGENCY CONTACT
_____

EMAIL:
_____

PHONE:
_____

ADDRESS:
_____

TRAINING

NEED
_____

EMPLOYEE NEEDS

NAME OF EMPLOYEE
_____

EMERGENCY CONTACT
_____

EMAIL:
_____

PHONE:
_____

ADDRESS:
_____

TRAINING
_____

NEED
_____

NAME OF EMPLOYEE
_____

EMERGENCY CONTACT
_____

EMAIL:
_____

PHONE:
_____

ADDRESS:
_____

TRAINING
_____

NEED
_____

NAME OF EMPLOYEE
_____

EMERGENCY CONTACT
_____

EMAIL:
_____

PHONE:
_____

ADDRESS:
_____

TRAINING
_____

NEED
_____

EMPLOYEE NEEDS

NAME OF EMPLOYEE
_____

EMERGENCY CONTACT
_____

EMAIL:
_____

PHONE:
_____

ADDRESS:
_____

TRAINING
_____

NEED
_____

NAME OF EMPLOYEE
_____

EMERGENCY CONTACT
_____

EMAIL:
_____

PHONE:
_____

ADDRESS:
_____

TRAINING
_____

NEED
_____

NAME OF EMPLOYEE
_____

EMERGENCY CONTACT
_____

EMAIL:
_____

PHONE:
_____

ADDRESS:
_____

TRAINING
_____

NEED
_____

EMPLOYEE NEEDS

NAME OF EMPLOYEE
_____

EMERGENCY CONTACT
_____

EMAIL:
_____

PHONE:
_____

ADDRESS:
_____

TRAINING
_____

NEED
_____

NAME OF EMPLOYEE
_____

EMERGENCY CONTACT
_____

EMAIL:
_____

PHONE:
_____

ADDRESS:
_____

TRAINING
_____

NEED
_____

NAME OF EMPLOYEE
_____

EMERGENCY CONTACT
_____

EMAIL:
_____

PHONE:
_____

ADDRESS:
_____

TRAINING
_____

NEED
_____

EMPLOYEE NEEDS

NAME OF EMPLOYEE
_____

EMERGENCY CONTACT
_____

EMAIL:
_____

PHONE:
_____

ADDRESS:
_____

TRAINING
_____

NEED
_____
_____

NAME OF EMPLOYEE
_____

EMERGENCY CONTACT
_____

EMAIL:
_____

PHONE:
_____

ADDRESS:
_____

TRAINING
_____

NEED
_____
_____

NAME OF EMPLOYEE
_____

EMERGENCY CONTACT
_____

EMAIL:
_____

PHONE:
_____

ADDRESS:
_____

TRAINING
_____

NEED
_____

Supplies- Shelter In Place

ITEM	QUANTITY	EXPIRATION
Food/People		
Food/Animals		
Bottled Water		
Battery Radio		
Flashlight		
AAA Batteries		
AA Batteries		
C Batteries		
D Batteries		
Cell Phone Chargers		
Plastic Sheeting		
Duct Tape		
Manual Can Opener		
Cell Phone Power Bank		
Blankets		

Supplies- Shelter In Place

ITEM	QUANTITY	EXPIRATION
Emergency Cash		
Mess Kits		
Sanitation Kits		
Fire Extinguisher		
Medications/Ice Packs		
Dust Masks Pets		
Dust Masks People		
Plastic Sheeting		
Duct Tape		
Manual Can Opener		
Cell Phone Power Bank		
Blankets		
Utility Wrench		

Supplies- Shelter In Place

ITEM	QUANTITY	EXPIRATION
Sanitation Supply Kits		
Hand Sanitizers		
Plastic Bags		
Baby Wipes		
5 Gallon Container		
Lid With Hole In Center Toilet Paper		
Disposable Mess Kits		
Paper Plates		
Plastic Utensils		
Plastic Cups		

Supplies-Evacuation

ITEM	QUANTITY	EXPIRATION
Baskets w/ Client's Information		
Employee Communications/ Head Counts		
Leads		
Muzzles		
Food To Go		
Water To Go		
Crates		
First Aid Kit		
Paper Maps		
Calming Tools		

Supplies-Evacuation

ITEM	QUANTITY	EXPIRATION

First Aid Kit- 1

ITEM	QUANTITY	EXPIRATION
Gauze		
Gauze Rolls		
Wound Cleanser Cat Safe		
Saline Solution		
Antibiotic Cream Cat Safe		
Digital Thermometer		
KY Jelly/Vaseline		
Surgurical Glue		
Vet Wrap		
Diphenhydramine		
Safety Pin		
Hydrogen Peroxide		
Activated Charcoal		
Tea Bags/Glucose Packets		
Muzzles		

First Aid Kit- 1

ITEM	QUANTITY	EXPIRATION
Tylenol/Advil/People		
Hemostatic Gauze		
Suture Strips		
Sam E splints		
Fold Up Litter		

First Aid Kit- 2

ITEM	QUANTITY	EXPIRATION
Gauze		
Gauze Rolls		
Wound Cleanser Cat Safe		
Saline Solution		
Antibiotic Cream Cat Safe		
Digital Thermometer		
KY Jelly/Vaseline		
Surgurical Glue		
Vet Wrap		
Diphenhydramine		
Safety Pin		
Hydrogen Peroxide		
Activated Charcoal		
Tea Bags/Glucose Packets		
Muzzles		

First Aid Kit- 2

ITEM	QUANTITY	EXPIRATION
Tylenol/Advil/People		
Hemostatic Gauze		
Suture Strips		
Sam E splints		
Fold Up Litter		

First Aid Kit- 3

ITEM	QUANTITY	EXPIRATION
Gauze		
Gauze Rolls		
Wound Cleanser Cat Safe		
Saline Solution		
Antibiotic Cream Cat Safe		
Digital Thermometer		
KY Jelly/Vaseline		
Surgurical Glue		
Vet Wrap		
Diphenhydramine		
Safety Pin		
Hydrogen Peroxide		
Activated Charcoal		
Tea Bags/Glucose Packets		
Muzzles		

First Aid Kit- 3

ITEM	QUANTITY	EXPIRATION
Tylenol/Advil/People		
Hemostatic Gauze		
Suture Strips		
Sam E splints		
Fold Up Litter		

HAZARD TYPES

1	**Chemical/Radiation**	
2	Civil Unrest	
3	Cyber	
4	Death Of Pet	
5	Dog Attack	
6	Earth Movement	
7	Groomer Safety	
8	Fire/Gas Leak	
9	Flood	
10	Heat	
11	Hurricane	
12	Medical Event	
13	Power Outtage	
14	Reputation	
15	Tornado	
16	Water Loss	
17	Winter	
18		
19		

CHEMICAL/RADIATION

1. Follow government recommendation to either evacuate or shelter in place.
2. If evacuating, follow standard evacuation protocols.
3. If shelter in place, set up vapor barrier on windows and doors in addition to standard shelter in place protocols.
4. Turn off HVAC systems.

CIVIL UNREST/ ACTIVE SHOOTER

1. Follow Shelter In Place Protocols
2. Follow Active Shooter Training Protocols
3. Lock doors
4. Call 911
5. Go to safe hiding place
6. If safe to do so or instructed by emergency responders, exit the building

CYBER

1. Contact credit cards and banks
2. Change passwords
3. Contact clients if personal info is compromised
4. Contact insurance company to start a claim
5. If a device has a virus, turn it off, and let an IT service handle it
6. Use your alternate system for processing clients and payments.

Prevention

1. Keep password list secure
2. Use 2 factor authorization
3. Back up devices on a regular basis
4. Use RFID Cases

DEATH OF PET

1. Secure all other pets in facility
2. Inform Team Leader
3. Collect client information including vet release
4. Contact vet
5. Contact owners with prepared statement with designated staff member
6. Transport pet to vet unless instructed otherwise by owner
7. Order and pay for necropsy report
8. Download and save to a specific drive folder all video
9. Inform insurance company
10. Inform business lawyer
11. Debrief staff
12. Prepare for reputation damage
13. Set up grief counseling/staff support

Prepared Statement

Hi, (Name Of Client), we regret to inform you that a medical incident has occured with (Name Of Pet). We will meet you at (Name And Address Of Vet.)

Preemptive Social Media Post

It is with great sadness, that (Name Of Pet) has passed in our care. Our trained staff did (What was done) and are devastated. We have ordered a necropsy report and hope to have answers soon.

DOG ATTACK

1. Secure and remove all pets not involved
2. Separate dogs or dog from person using techniques from aggressive dog training
3. Secure aggressive pet
4. Call 911 if person is injured
5. Contact vet if pet is injured
6. Call emergency contacts for injured parties
7. Begin treatment for injuries
8. Contact insurance company

EARTH MOVEMENT

1. If inside stay inside
2. Take pets off of grooming tables
3. Secure pets in lower kennel crates
4. Turn off utilities
5. Prepare for aftershocks
6. Follow evacuation protocols
7. If in Tsunami zone, take pets and staff to higher ground.

FIRE/GAS LEAK

1. Evacuate as practiced, take pets to secure location outside of building & secure pets.
2. Take basket of that days paperwork
3. Call 911 from safe location
4. Contact Team Leader
5. Contact owners
6. Turn off utilities if able
7. DO NOT at any point, try to go back inside if building is on fire.

FLOOD

1. Turn off utilities
2. Place important business equipment, paperwork, and tools as high as possible
3. Follow evacuation protocols

Miscellanaeous
   1. If you are in a known flood zone, or are within close proximity of a river or dam area, it is advised to have inflatable boats for emergency evacuation.

PET PROFESSIONAL SAFETY

1. Set up your Buddy system/mutual aid contact
2. Know where your exits are
3. Have an unobstructed path to the exit
4. Trust your gut
5. Check sex offender registry
6. Decide on personal protection and take recommended training
7. Have a list of excuses ready to not enter a home

Sample Excuse

I have a family emergency and will call you to reschedule.

HEAT-PET

1.Cool off pet with active cooling by pouring tepid water over the pet's body and place animal in front of fan.

2. Make sure to stop active cooling measures once the body hits 103 degrees (use digital thermometer to monitor). The body will continue to cool on its own at that point, if active cooling continues, it may cause the body to go into hypothermia.

3. Contact vet for further instructions and to prepare for your arrival

4. Prepare pet for transport. Bring client signed waivers

5. Contact owners to meet at vet

6. Watch for factors such as shock or seizures

Remember, heat stroke is life threatening so fast action is necessary. Heat stroke causes the body to lose it's ability to further regulate its temperature causing the core temperature to continue to rise.

HEAT-PEOPLE

1.Cool off person by removing as much clothing as possible

2. Contact 9-1-1 (heat stroke) or urgent care (heat exhaustion) for further instructions

3. Start active cooling the patient by pouring tepid water over the patient's body and place cold packs in armpits, sides of neck, back of knees, and in groin area

4. Prepare person to transport to urgent care or wait for 9-1-1 to arrive. If self transport, bring any employee documents as needed.

5. Contact emergency contact to meet at urgent care

6. Monitor the patient for other factors such as shock or seizures

Remember, heat stroke is life threatening so fast action is necessary. Heat stroke causes the body to lose it's ability to further regulate its temperature causing the core temperature to continue to rise.

HURRICANES

1. Make sure generator has gas, also check & fill additional gas containers
2. Protect electronic equipment and client info if possible duplicate in cloud storage
3. Turn off and unplug all electric equipment.
4. Turn off utilities.
5. Board up windows and doors
6. Add sandbags
7. Bring in outside loose objects.
8. Follow shelter in place protocol unless evacuation is advised/instructed

MEDICAL EVENT

1. Contact 911
2. Assess medical concern and provide appropriate First aid or CPR (AED if available)
3. Contact Team Leader
4. Prepare for ambulance or transport to urgent care
5. .Contact emergency contact for person

POWER OUTTAGE

1. Unplug sensitive electronics such as computers
2. Contact utility company, NOT 911
3. Contact owners to pick up pets
4. Evaluate use of generator and sanitary issues (fill water containers to be able to flush toilets)

REPUTATION

1. Review video footage and secure to separate drive folder of issue in question
2. Choose one of your pre-prepared statements
3. Contact attorney and insurance company

TORNADOES

1. Evacuate if ordered to do so.
2. If there is not time, move all pets, staff, and clients to designated safe area in building.
3. Contact owners
4. If unable to contact owners, place pets in safe secure area or contact mutual aid if needed.

WATER LOSS

1. Finish up pets in tub with stored bottled water
2. Finish up pets that have already had their bath.
3. Contact owners to pick up pets that can not be bathed and contact to reschedule clients who were on the schedule to come in.

WINTER

1. Keep warm, review prevention tips if using heating equipment (ie: space heaters)
2. Minimize heat loss from building from drafts by covering windows and doors with insulation kits.
3. Wrap exposed pipes and let water dribble
4. Contact owners for pick up
5. If owners are unable to pick up pets, proceed with shelter in place or contact mutual aid help

INITIAL
DEBRIEFING

DATE

_____

WHAT HAPPENED

_____

HOW DID IT HAPPEN

_____

_____

_____

HOW WAS THE INCIDENT HANDLED

_____

_____

_____

_____

_____

_____

_____

_____

INITIAL
DEBRIEFING

WHAT COULD'VE BEEN DONE DIFFERENTLY

_____

_____

_____

_____

IS THERE ANYTHING ADDITIONAL
MEMBERS INVOLVED WOULD LIKE TO
DISCUSS

_____

_____

_____

_____

_____

_____

_____

STAFF NEEDS

_____

_____

_____

_____

SECONDARY DEBRIEFING

DATE
_____

WHAT HAPPENED
_____

HOW DID IT HAPPEN
_____
_____
_____
_____

HOW WAS THE INCIDENT HANDLED
_____
_____
_____
_____
_____
_____
_____
_____
_____
_____

SECONDARY DEBRIEFING

HOW COULD THIS HAVE BEEN PREVENTED

_____

_____

_____

_____

WHAT COULD WE HAVE DONE BETTER

_____

_____

_____

_____

_____

_____

_____

STAFF NEEDS

_____

_____

_____

EVACUATION PROTOCOL

1. Contact Team Leader
2. Place important client and business info into portable container along with go bag and place in car
3. Help clients to their vehicles with their pet
4. Place pets securely in vehicles
5. Drive pets to designated emergency animal shelter or to mutual aid help
6. Contact owners to let them know where their pets are
7. Turn off breakers and utilities place sign in window about evacuation if applicable
8. Text SHELTER plus your zipcode to 43362

SHELTER IN PLACE PROTOCOL

1. Announce 1 minute to doors locking
2. Lock doors and windows
3. Place sign in window
4. Bring secured pets/people to designated safe room
5. Gather supplies
6. Follow instructions from authorities
7. Call owners regarding pets
8. Allow staff and clients to call home

Resources

Local/County Emergency Management Office

FEMA.gov

Ready.Gov

Fire Department

Continuing Education Programs

Upcoming Training

Human First Aid

Pet First Aid

Emergency Preparedness Drills

CERT Training

Emergency/Disaster Preparation Workshops

Separating Dogs While Attacking/Fighting Workshops

How To Do A Thorough Nose To Tail Workshop

Recovery

Take Pictures

Contact Insurance

Assess Damage

Fill Out FEMA Forms

Keep Employees Abreast

Turn utilities back on if no structual damage occurred

Check up on pets brought to shelter.

How will you get back to work

Contact repair service providers

DAMAGED

- ☐
- ☐
- ☐
- ☐
- ☐
- ☐
- ☐
- ☐
- ☐
- ☐
- ☐
- ☐

- ☐
- ☐
- ☐
- ☐
- ☐
- ☐
- ☐
- ☐
- ☐
- ☐
- ☐
- ☐

SUPPLIER LIST

COMPANY

PRODUCT

EMAIL:

PHONE:

ADDRESS:

COMPANY

PRODUCT

EMAIL:

PHONE:

ADDRESS:

COMPANY

PRODUCT

EMAIL:

PHONE:

ADDRESS:

COMPANY

PRODUCT

EMAIL:

PHONE:

ADDRESS:

CHECK IN PROCEDURES

1	**Print Out Waivers And Checklists For Client**	
2	Have Client Acknowledge Information Is Still Correct	
3	Perform Check in Procedure	
4	Gum Color	
5	No Ear/Eye/ Nose Discharge	
6	Walks Normally	
7	Alert	
8	No Apparent Pain Response	
9	Teeth are good	
10	New Medcal Concerns	
11	Medications	
12	Place waivers and checklists in a to go basket on front desk	
13		
14		
15		
16		
17		
18		
19		

INTAKE PROTOCOLS

1. Print out updated client information, including rabies status and signed waivers
2. Have clients acknowledge information is correct
3. Do thorough full body, from head to tail assessment and note gum color and any discharge
4. Place all signed paperwork in the to go container at reception
5. Make sure pet is secure and there is one pet a time in the reception area or on the ground

Maintenance Schedule

ITEM	DATE	SIGNED
Outlets		
Dryer Vents		
HVAC Filters		

Maintenance Schedule

ITEM	DATE	SIGNED
Outlets		
Dryer Vents		
HVAC Filters		

Sample Waivers- All Need To Signed And Dated By Owner Annually

In the event of a suspected heart stoppage, I authorize/do not authorize (Name Of Business) to perform CPR.

In the event of a medical emergency, I authorize (Name Of Business) to provide first aid techniques and to transport to veterinarian.

In the event of an emergency in which (Name Of Business) is ordered to either evaluate or shelter in place, I authorize (Name Of Business) to assume guardianship until such time I can safely take possession of my pets.

*It is recommended that any client forms and waivers be reviewed by a business lawyer in your state.

Need Help Filling This Workbook Out? Then Join This Facebook Group